D1082491

Vanishing Acts

Vanishing Acts
MOIRA MACDOUGALL

PEDLAR PRESS | ST. JOHN'S

For information, write Pedlar Press at
113 Bond Street, St John's NL A1C 1T6 Canada

COVER ART   Michael Pittman, *Obstruction #4 (ablution)*, mixed media on panel, 2008.
DESIGN   Mark Byk
TYPEFACE   Ogg & Rosart
EDITORIAL   John Glenday
Printed in Canada at Coach House Printing, Toronto ON

LIBRARY AND ARCHIVES CANADA CATALOGUING IN PUBLICATION
MacDougall, Moira, author
Vanishing acts / Moira MacDougall.

Poems.
ISBN 978-1-897141-94-6 (softcover)

I. TITLE.

PS8625.D78V36 2019   C811'.6   C2018-906545-1
First Edition

ACKNOWLEDGEMENTS
The publisher wishes to thank the Canada Council for the Arts and the NL Publishers Assistance Program for their generous support of our publishing program.

Canada Council   Conseil des arts
for the Arts   du Canada

Newfoundland
Labrador

... I guess it never ends. A brother never ends. I prowl him. He does not end.
—Anne Carson

Contents

PART 1

Alphabet: All the Ways We Can Vanish	15
Vanishing	16
Vanishing 2	18
Note to Antigone — #1	19
Family Frenzy	21
Surrender Like a Camel	23
Thought for the Day — #1	24
At My Brother's Bedside	26
Flip of a Coin	27
See How Swiftly	28
Flight	29
Thought for the Day — #2	30
Boreal Lungs	31
The Book Launch	32
A Mother's Love	33
Train Rides, You & I	35

PART 2

I Wish That Hills and Mountains Were Behind Me?	42
Shanks, Femurs & Shoulder Blades	43
Island Song: Captiva	45
Thought for the Day — #3	46
Wing	48
Elegy for Nan	49
Tsunami Blues	51
A Prickle of Porcupines	52
Thought for the Day — #4	53
Lips Cool	55
Thanksgiving Weekend Burials	56

Note to Antigone — #2   57
First Christmas with Everyone Gone   58
Paidos-Paraleipsis   59
Thought for the Day — #5   60

PART 3

List, Lists, Listing   65
Grief in Hand   67
Bird Song   69
Animals Go Down   70
All the Tender Things   71
Yoga Hangover   73
Fate Turns, Santa Domingo, DR   74
Diagnosis: Thanatosis   75
Under the Milkweed   77
Spring Thaw   78
Note to Antigone — #3   79

PART 4

Fates At Work   82
Flesh & Bone   83
On the Road to Damascus   85
Thought for the Day — #6   86
Cornstalks in the First Freeze   88
Rituals of Hair — Preparations   89
Rituals of Hair — Buying the Wig   91
Invisible   92
Star Wars   94
It Happens Overhead or By Your Foot   95
Hillside Relics   97

Thought for the Day — #7   98
Rituals of Hair — The Cancer Ride   99
Note to Antigone — #4   100
Relish   101

PART 5

Something Has Bitten Deep   104
Rituals of Hair — Reciprocity   105
Rosedale Valley Commute   107
Cluster Fuck   109
Will It Ever Stop   110
Note to Antigone — #5   111
Thought for the Day — #8   112
Become the Sky   113
You Can Have It All   115
Final Thought — Prowling   116

PART 6

Fate's Fate — A Response to Antigonick   121
— Let Me Try Again   122
— Third Time's a Charm?   123
— Does a Fourth Response Make It Whole?   124

Notes   127
Acknowledgements   129
Bibliography   131

PART 1

Alphabet: All the Ways We Can Vanish

Abandon
Abdicate
Abscond
Absent
Absorb

Blind
Break
Burn
Bury
Burrow

Camouflage
Cease
Collapse
Cover
Crumble
Cut
Crush

Decamp
Decay
Decline
Degenerate
Descend
Devour
Die
Diminish
Disappear
Disguise
Disintegrate
Dismantle
Disperse
Dissipate
Dissolve
Drape
Drift
Drown
Dwindle

Ebb
Empty
End
Enfold
Erode
Escape
Evacuate
Evaporate
Exile
Exit
Expire

Fade
Faint
Fall
Fizzle
Flatten
Flee
Flight
Fly
Fold
Fray

Grind

Hide

Illusion
Invisible

Lapse
Leak
Lean
Leave
Lose

Melt
Migrate

Perish
Poison

Quaff
Quit

Radiate
Recede
Reincarnate
Relinquish
Remove
Resign
Rot

Scatter
Secede
Seep
Sift
Sink
Slip
Snip
Split
Stray
Subside
Swaddle
Sweep

Thaw
Tiptoe
Tumble

Unravel

Vacate
Vamoose
Vaporize

Wane
Wilt
Withdraw
Wither

Vanishing

On a bender here, tumbling down
a prairie dog hole into a maze, catch
a whiff, pungent as elephant spoor.
Dung beetles roll frayed neurons into a ball:

yes, it's all shit. Random shit. The world keeps
turning. Deep time. No time. Shadfly existence:
here and gone within twenty-four hours,
our wings splayed over a verandah light bulb

or hung to dry on the cottage's blue siding
we mistook for sky. Lace-like, we slip
between grass blades, baptism by garden hose.
Reincarnation for the western mind.

Tumble

Slip

Reincarnation

Vanishing (2)

Thing is, I stumbled across Anne Carson's
Antigonick in the midst of mourning the loss
of my older brother, baby sister, father, beloved dog —
practically all at once, before finding myself

ill, my sister-in-law more so. Then husband.
Not to bring the whole Greek affair down
on your head but Tig's story echoes
throughout my years — older brother by my side.

His near drowning on the Mediterranean made
Odysseus' journey palpable. Greek gods,
male *and* female, animal and bird, riveting.
Curled in his hammock as the main mast broke,

oblivion drew close. The desert god we'd known
evaporated. OK, confess: born into a household
where theology is milk and manna, dad's a lawyer
becomes clergy — anybody else's rituals of worship,

intriguing. Tonight, sitting in grief's debris,
will someone knock me out? No life but for sleep
and meals. Will I live all this loss again with age?

Descent on a spiral staircase, steps
erode beneath me. Suck-hole of tears.
Antigone closed the door behind her.
My dear brother, your death only the beginning.

Note to Antigone — #1

Dear Tig:

You were there the whole time in plain sight. Why I should find
you now, forty years later, as Carson calls you up, out of the grave,
out of the backwaters of my memory? You haven't aged a bit!

This, in spite of all those white men crawling over your memory,
squeezing their life from you — Hegel, Holderin, Kant, Kierkegaard,
Nietzsche. They put you on par with Jesus — ah, right — a man after
your time who caused a furor of thought, indeed a revolution that
swept the world!

Having been steeped in Aeschylus, Euripides, your Sophocles,
Shakespeare, impressed with how you stood up to Creon,
sacrificing yourself to do right by your gods, your family.

You spoke, but you didn't live. I couldn't take another after Anna,
Emma, Virginia, Anne Sexton. How is suicide the only narrative?
How is it that authors so consistently kill off the feminine?

I fell prey — unrequited love for a married man when I was seventeen.
Wanted to die. Shocked, I survived. No script for the next chapter.

Thirty years later, writing my first collection of poems, you were
simply a solitary young woman trying to figure out how to speak to
a culture where our silence is preferred, where our fathers define
our stories.

My dad was no royal figure, but a priest in a small northern town
where everyone watched, commented like a Greek chorus, waiting
for you to fall. I did not disappoint.

Drown

Evaporate

Erode

Five breasts, a prostate, a liver
my brother's bones, Cancer's wild dogs
circle my family: they feed on and on, frenzied.
Stunned by the speed of mounting losses, I turn toward
Mom who resists the undertow but is losing inches. We
grow eye to eye standing in the kitchen, making tea.
What is ahead? Bereft as clam shells rolling
onto shore, ground to dust by lovers'
feet, we are humbled to a speck.
Spindly sandpipers peck
their forked toes
my grave.

Devour

Grind

Die

On her knees, thighs hot as desert sands
press into the studio wall. She opens
her breastbone to the sky, breaking light
as she incarnates your lines. Thistle to cloth
fingers hook around ankles to complete
the arc — heat surges from quads rippling
a flock of starlings as they swoon. Sternum
lifts she burns, mutters small prayers
as sandstorms of brother, sister, father
blow through her heart. All dust.
Mercy, she cries, as her legs fold under.

I am a strange new kind of
inbetween thing aren't I, not at home with the
dead
nor with the living.

—Anne Carson

Creon had his word of the day: law, family, order. Our family breakfasts focused on resurrection, eternity, immortality, infinity, oblivion. These touchstones made time elastic, loose as the band of my grandmother's underwear, blinding us to molecular degeneration, to tattered endings.

All that desire strung along the communion table our father hosted: sanitized, crisp with starch. And yet I wished *it* again and again as the three lay wedged between treatment and death. And *it* did. End. All within a year.

Hope is a frayed thread you pick off your mother's sweater. You are never prepared, however probable: it is a blow. Reflexively you bow.

Break

Burn

Degenerate

At My Brother's Bedside

Something's wrong — brain-in-my-gut emitting
distress signals the day before first book launch.
Find you actively dying? Your numbers crashing,
we were hoping for a last summer. I'd crawl in bed

beside you, one hug to hold a lifetime.
Tröstet, tröstet meine Lieben.

Your youngest daughter is tucked in your arms.
The past too far back. The bed too small. Holding
your Odyssian quad — a blood clot loosens from
its wounded moorings, a peony blossoming

in your lungs. Fierce as walrus tusks, oxygen tubes
howl a north wind over your tundra cheeks —
you cannot hear us in the blizzard. I freeze.
Mute, behind my Jackie-O demeanor.

Don't think I'm gonna make your launch party.
My twin, my rock, against whose loss I break
sure as your sailboat on the Mediterranean.
Oh, how we fancied our quest for truth

more rigorous than our father's — it was.
For him, God was all heart — we burrowed on,
pericope by pericope, through the tunnel
of his dogma, past textual criticism into eastern light.

And yet, every Christmas, every Easter, Bach.
Python-esque quips pepper the air
as period instruments vibrate off sanctuary walls.
Did we ever travel far from home?

my love of you burnished silver
with envy as the Bluenose rides
unpolished waters.

Toss and flip:

the lush canopy of your love absorbs
too-bright sun, but even our mom
knew your death shadowed
the sapling-poems I'd seeded.
(It's not as if you chose the time.)

Toss and flip:

my love of you, burnished in the light
shines, slips into silver waters.

See How Swiftly

In the catacombs of a hospital's back stairs
our bond loosens. I race between the slips
of dying siblings. You die knowing your death
is not the end. Our sister is one floor above.

Her loneliness a wind tossing us
upon the waters, she rolls onto the beach
of her hospital bed. We lie thigh by thigh
as if sunbathing, holding hands.

Do people think I am dying? She missed
this last storm in the ER, you and I,
her inflated buoys. *Funny, I am in no pain.*
Your death, a parting gift: she witnesses

your last breath, sees how swiftly
a blizzard dissipates.

As she senses another storm approaching, my sister
calls. It is 1AM. We rush to the ER.
A lull in the usual chaos, we are afforded private space.
Knees to chest, a soft keening rises
from her throat as the disease tunnels from liver to bones
the soft hillsides of breast already shorn.
Into our second night I forage the hallways for blankets,
rolling one into a pillow, the other
for camouflage. Through chrome safety bars we hold hands,
"It's kind of like we are on an overseas flight," she whispers.

9.9 million Internet citations for Infinity
15 million for Resurrection
24.1 million on Eternity
Oblivion, 30.9 million
Fear is primal: 600 million and counting...

.

That I might drink and leave this world unseen,
And with thee fade into the forest dim.
—Keats

North to the lake in search of reprieve,
only envy walking the forest trails — a deciduous tree,
unfurling into the broadest expanse of light, twists
its spine, veins infused blue, then yellow rays,
knows green until earth tips north and ethylene
is released — sleep is on its way! It will not feel Winter's bite.

I cannot sleep, I cannot sleep — neither the comfort of my dog,
nor crisp boreal air, scent of burning cedar, deep bath.
I twist and turn, night to night.

Fade far away, dissolve and quite forget
What thou amongst the leaves have never known

The last battalion of yellow jackets circle
glass of red wine emitting signals of warmth, sweet.
An occasional crow and gull heard over the golden orbs
of leaves

... [my] dull brain perplexes and retards.

On the third morning, wind dies. Frost
is a caravan of insects scratching in the tall grass
dispersed in tangerine light.

The Book Launch

Promising to return that evening, *I'll read*
for both of us. Read for yourself, you whisper
in rebuke. Salinger's Zooey to my Franny.
I step up to the mic — a wine glass shatters

on the patio stone, my legs waver in the crest
of your drowning. Gripping the podium, I won't
say your name — it will sink me. *What should*
our parents have done? Be with you, their eldest son,

sedated in his last hours? Witness their daughter's
literary debut? Our sister, skin yellow as sulphur,
wheels herself to your room.

Huddling sheep in a pen, silent but for occasional
bleats, sobs, we wander to and from your bedside.
Lie with you. Our father calls me urgently.
You were terrific tonight, honey.

Winds blow, thunder cracks, lightning pulses.
Olympus welcoming you home? Stupefied,
fingers tap games of Solitaire.

Your wife in surgery two weeks later.
Same hospital. Two floors up. We, drown-proof.
Laugh recalling the arrival of police at your memorial —
friends of yours? Ha! Liquor license to be suspended

if we don't reduce numbers. African drums pound
a warrior's rhythm. I read a Hindu *situ.* Tears
boulders on the path. Stumble.

for a first born son is sacrosanct.
There was no competition,
but I played on. You carried
the trophy, wary of siblings who
distracted her adoring eyes.
Made myself small, tucked
at your side, hoping her warmth
might graze my shoulder.

Dissolve

Dissipate

Flight

There we are: you in your shirt and tie, me
in my new winter coat with its raccoon fur collar,
trying to look as old as you. The porter

helps us aboard, the small folds of his palm
pink on the other side of dark flesh. Names us
Bruce-y and Lucy as he hoists up the metal stairs.

The chaos of our small lives is hushed. Parents
recede, disappear. Down narrow, rocking corridors
we lurch and lean toward the glass dome car.

Ice cubes tinkle in glasses as strangers
swirl their drinks, smoke curling around
their lips, silver as the curve of the club car,

up steep, carpeted steps, we slip into plush seats
as the roof opens to sky, to endless frames of bush.
The flick of a deer's tail as it disappears, blue jays,

cardinals, crows. Too soon hunger rumbles.
We leap over grinding hitches, sparks flare, rails
laid bare — the lurching platform

a monster's jaw and I am nearly swallowed
as winter's fury inhales the train's stale breath.
Safe again, we unfold used wax paper to our mom's

turkey sandwiches and shortbreads. Two rounds
of Crazy Eights, what Christmas gifts await
at our grandparents? We speculate:

a record player, a gold bracelet. The whistle sings,
the clickety-clack sway swings, heads lurch
then rest as the landscape folds in around us...

One last ride? Growing old together, a child's dream.
Today, train tracks to the east, commuter trains
rumble by. You rest beneath a Linden tree.

Hawks circle overhead.
Alone, I rock with the rhythm, waiting to arrive.

Abandon

Abdicate

Abscond

Absorb

Absent

Blind

Break

Burn

Bury

Burrow

PART 2

Escape

Fall

Strip

I Wish That Hills and Mountains Were Behind Me?

Our sister's brief reprieve is over. Her lover
takes her home. The day I am accepted at Banff,
she asks if I would cruise with her to England.

What to do? Pursue a dream of a lifetime,
or accompany my sister on her last journey?
You won't like my answer.

All that was not said — my need for escape,
her need to live to the very end;
our inability to speak of a *last* journey.

She was hoping for more chemo.
No ripping this bandage from her heart.
Mom travels with her as I nestle into the spine

of the continent, pour my loss of you into
the constraints of an elegy. Vertebrae by vertebrae,
the slope in her back steepens. Sends boyfriend

cycling through the Rockies. Won't hear
of his staying... climbing, climbing.
What was he to do? Eternally bonded in our regret.

Guess you fell through the ice upstream, plunging
between ragged crevices in early spring.
Now open to the sky on a granite shard,

scavengers have stripped you to bright bone.
Your Chiclet teeth sift mud by the riverbank
twenty feet from your torso. Microbial communities

gather for shelter along your antlers. Hot
instinct surges to stroke your still-furred shank
to cradle your broken jaw. Restraint redoubles

as I pass your carcass on the road,
femur upright, red as a traffic signal I circle round.
Winged scavengers have yet to feast,

though nostrils are cooling by the whir of flies.
Retrieving your shoulder blade from the riverbed,
lichen, a speckle meadow and river transforming

bone to bed. Fragile as a Spanish fan you perch
on my desk, mountain winds blow cold. Staring
through an oval window, four deer are lifted

by rope and pulley from an icy pond. Alive.
I embrace your bones, an ossuary of love.

Erode

Drift

Sift

Island Song: Captiva

Sea oats rattle as they brown
stiff-stemmed. Seed clasped to seed,

a meticulously plaited head of hair
tenacious against the callous breeze

that lifts a song of bones from the sea
as they roll, lull, rub, erode.

Once homes to small muscles of life,
they surface in the jaws of dogged waves.

The ghost of a dolphin figured in a drift
of sand, swims.

Thought for the Day — #3

'One day at a time' is a wicked, wicked philosophy by which to
live! You keep your head down, focus on the next meal, the next
nap, the next clinic. She wants you beside her on the bed, holding
hands, not flapping around the ward looking for doctors — most
know the limits of their knowing — and she doesn't want to know.
It is her life, her dying. Chartreuse, she is alive, upright as an orchid.

Die

Stir

Sweep

Wing

One Friday morning at home, as she wanted,
our baby sister dies. Family on their way
to visit — *not* in the nick of time — ten minutes

too late, to be precise. Just right?
In her lover's arms, one last surge
of the internal ocean, she is swept away.

No arrangements. We walk to Dignity Burials
advertising *Funerals for Less* — no credit cards,
no cheques, scurry to bank machines,

attendant counts the cash at the kitchen table.
Gathering on the porch as they carry her to their van,
a monarch butterfly passes over. Only the moon could

compete for banality and yet, emailing her oncologist,
he writes he is in Japan at a conference and paying homage
to the Mizuko Jizo, thinking of us. Small statues honour

the soul of a lost child. He'd read my poem of the same title,
has a stone-rubbing of one in his living room. Flutter
of a butterfly's wing stirs a heart overseas.

The thrum of the ship's engines, wind, waves
crest and fall, we are supple as a sea monster.

Crab-like, I lurch toward the dining room.
Stiletto heels, a sand-piper's footprint on the carpet.

A rose on my table vibrates, white Xmas berries
shake, we surge — a semaphore of the roiling vortex

that enfolds us. Eighteen hundred other spirits
ride alongside as endless bolts of tulled-water froth,

fold over our path. How could I not remember
declining to join you at sea just before you died —

a strum of regret, another sip of wine.

Decline

Resign

Fold

We land in Cancun pursuing northern visions of sun-water-tan,
but you scan the beach, the camera of your eye rolling
as breakers tenderize the sand, noting this strip
is five hundred metres wide, not a six metre palm in sight.

The Gonâve Microplate extending from here to Haiti,
we resign to the blue of Caribbean waters,
margaritas whetting the appetite for more.
Three days, red flags crack the air while sun shines,
sunscreen, hat, sandals all line up at the foot of the chaise lounge.

A four hundred page novel tethers my attention, until whistles blow:
young lifeguards pull a man from the surf, limp. They pump,
yell, his bluing body, the widow's grief. Averting my eyes, skylines
offer no reprieve. My only latitude, fingers on the trembling page.

A Prickle of Porcupines

Archives of grief I see falling upon this house...
                                        —Anne Carson

It was as if you and she had found each other
then swam to retrieve our father
as he wandered the beach of the inland sea.
Ah, right, you missed the stroke he suffered

the day we were to bury your ashes. Illegally
in the park you had walked your dog
amongst wild grasses and hawks. Deep
in the crevices of his withering mind,

Dad knew your light had gone out, our sister dead.
Baby brother and I sit vigil — thigh to thigh
with the dear man who carried me
during his sojourn from law to theology.

Now his midwife as life's last portal opens.
We are a prickle of porcupines, roadside at night.

Thought for the Day — #4

Dying is hard labour, even when carried by the lightness of love.
It can go on and on, hours, days, weeks, months; or a different kind
of work awaits when you are unexpectedly plunged to the ocean floor.
The fantasy that is hospital TV. Daily life, the burden of redundancy.

Bury

Stroke

Wither

curves   *shimmer and undulate*

in morning sun

a salmon of electric green

juts from a sea of dull rock

lifting from the shelf   *we swim*

past the marketplace   *away from inspecting eyes*

in this small eddy of light   *my father's lips*

move ever so gently   *searching*

the rim of his universe   *for air*

Thanksgiving Weekend Burials

We bury Nan and Dad by the inland sea

                    our family's anchor for fifty years

Christians in the family insist on singing
                        Dad's favourite hymn

Jesus Loves Me, over their grave

                  without the minor chords
                    of his jazz keyboard.

                           Please stop.

Note to Antigone — #2

Dear Tig:

Thinking of you and your brother's broken body outside the
city wall as we bury my brother's ashes in a public park under a
Linden tree. A year later we discover the area ploughed over to
make way for a new hiking trail. His remains lost. That's the risk
when you play outside the rules.

First Christmas with Everyone Gone

Solace is Tafelmusik's *Messiah*.
Sustaining our annual tradition, bows of wood
line the concert hall, the soft strings sail me
into the great Ark. Opening words, a rip-tide.

Tröstet, tröstet meine Lieben.

Paidos—Paraleipsis
for Isobel

… hear remnants of eclipse, the sun
folds. Three crosses hang flesh, our tribal
tattoo. Abba, Abba restore the light!
Orphans all of us.

… rhyme with ellipsis, three marks on the page
step into white grief. 'Widowed' she howls,
finds her place.

… the patter of her children's footsteps
on the path to the beach

… abandoned on this side, her heart thrust back
under the wing of her scapula. It bends as she
relinquishes her children. No noun. No howl.
Sea gulls cry.

See why I think Antigone had it easy?
She was caught between two competing brothers.
Me too! Yes, she'd seen her father pluck out his own eyes,
but she had the gods' assurance she was doing right.

No homecare for her while wrangling a job, husband,
home and friends.

What do you do with grief in a random age?

Camouflage

Cease

Collapse

Cover

Crumble

Cut   Decamp

Crush   Decay

                       Decline

                       Degenerate

                       Descend

                       Devour

                       Die

                       Diminish

                       Disappear

                       Disguise

                       Disintegrate

                       Dismantle

                       Disperse

                       Dissipate

                       Dissolve

                       Drape

                       Drown

                       Dwindle

PART 3

Bless the rituals of a day that stay
the abyss, or at least until later
when all the things I need to do,
which if not done before I enter the day,

I never do: green tea, yoga, vitamins,
make the bed, hit the treadmill, shower and
get dressed. Ready for a nap, but we're out
the door by 8AM — it's foundation at Woodbine,

lipstick on the Lakeshore, mascara
up the Don Valley. (Consider what time
the Dali Lama would have to rise
if he had hair and makeup to apply!)

By Rosedale Road, I am complete, ready
for work — emails, phone calls, meetings
and reports. It's hard to believe a thought
for the abyss could compete. End of day,

oh my, no time for the abyss today
(thank god). There's groceries, dinner,

a dog to walk, family, friends, committee
meetings. Bless my husband, he loves to weed!

It's only Monday night,
help, I need a pen! Before I list and drown!

Ash

Loss

Fade

is a list, a prop. Clock ticks,
we talk forty-five minutes. No drift.
No dawdle. Paper wilts, soggy
with sweat, ink seeps tears
not shared for fear of more loss.
Grief over flame wavering: I am ash.

Drown

Seep

Wilt

Would you indulge me? Please, sit in your leather chair
and out of view, let me lie on the couch, and would you

song-say my name with your soft Scottish brogue,
those rolling r-r-r-s that feel as if the alphabet rolls

into a ball of fine wool, the upright Anglo "oi" and "rah"
sheered to a moor hill we roll down, as my grandmother's

light cadence echoes beneath your voice, carries us on.
Please, just say it once more like the ruby red kinglet
calling for his mate. Call me home.

Animals Go Down

As your birthday approaches, we put Sienna down,
ailing standard poodle, my closest companion
of fifteen years. Our vet offers me four doors.
Will this not end? I can open any one or none.

The modern Sphinx: I choose none, pay the bill.
Return three days later. Thought the timing
Biblical though resurrection unlikely.
Your dear border collie follows.

We rearrange the living room furniture
so a morning's descent isn't a daily confrontation
with absence.

Always had a soft spot for Galileo, his failure
of courage that saved him from the wall, a bench,
whatever they used to pin a heretic down,

then twist, pinch, burn or slice out a confession.
Severed fingers abandoned on the page
light a galaxy of terror as my young animus
is asked to give up his ring finger late one night.

No, no, I am no fictional protagonist,
war hero or saint, yet an audible Yes *passes*
my lips as a young soldier wheels himself out

before the cameras: he could survive without legs
he explains, but to be given transplanted arms was
to live again: the muzzle of my dog, my sister's last hug.
We race through the corridor to your bed. Hold tight.

Blind

Burn

Descent

It was only an hour. Single shots
of dog, caterpillar, eagle, cow,
camel and pigeon — not one too many

unless of course you are out of practice.
Me, pinned like a butterfly by the sacrum to the bed.
Dread's weight — coiled around my ribs —
dismantled one animal at a time as they parade

kneading lungs, liver, my overactive mind.
No churning stomach, no headache threatening
to crack the skull: lost in a cloud of sheets. Eternity tiptoes.

Fate turns, Santa Domingo, DR

Friday, 5PM, at a bar with colleagues
and cell phone rings. My dear GP insists I see her
Monday, 4PM. You know this is never good.

Without twitch of breath, what life is left
is camouflaged as death. She pulls
the cashmere throw up, over her head
like fiddlehead fronds recoiling
from a forager's blade. Round grows
rounder, heavier, green as the arc is steep.
It isn't depression, though the feeling low
gravity circling, drawing her close. No resisting
earth gives way to grief. Like the fire-bellied toad
tosses her head back, limbs splayed, limp on a leaf
keeping predators at bay. Holds her breath, waits.

Camouflage

Dismantle

Tiptoe

Under the Milkweed
For Danna

Hear the diagnosis. Lean forward, a violinist
awaiting her cue. Ask doctor to repeat, count,
forsaking breath, adrenals unleash frenzy.

Struck still, the small animal asks again: words
a slow-release poison slipping under the door.
Altered state. Make carrot ginger soup, sleep.

Perch on the balcony to shimmer of water, murmur
of trees, count swans and chickadees. Knit one,
purl two, tension wrong, unravel. Start again.

Wander the beach, see the doctor wave from
her cabin porch. Can't read her face.
Wave, turn and carry on. Steps quicken, breath

seizes as a storm builds — head to the dunes
for shelter. A sea of flannel sheets, I waken:
a chrysalis under the milkweed.

Spring Thaw

Fifty years sifting sand and sun with Mom
on this beach. Plans to travel together
have to wait. *Damn,* she cries! Wrap
my arm around her, reassure the diagnosis
is not as dire... yes, *sixth* one ill. Sandbags
on the riverbank before spring thaw.
Seems she stacked them months before.
Didn't help. Grief's current crushes like ice.

Note to Antigone — #3

Dear Tig:

Confess, wondering if you are my next gate of hell opening?
Having passed through religious orthodoxy, the crucible of
western culture and female sexuality; abandoned my art to
play twenty-five years of snakes and ladders in institutions of
all kinds — private, public, charitable — places women were
forbidden to enter in your time until I thought I was going to
be institutionalized! LOL.

Yes, even when you are allowed through the gate and find your
voice, you can fall prey to madness, because they still won't listen.

Found my art again! Achieved ISBN immortality. Then, promptly
exiled to the Land of Malady, the County of Cancer. The *Empress
of All Maladies* is one hard-ass bitch of a queen to serve.

Endless conversations with our modern priests of the mind
trying to stave off paralyzing fear of oblivion.

Ebb

Empty

End

Enfold

Erode

Escape

Evacuate

Evaporate

Exile   Fade

Exit   Faint

Expire   Fall

                         Fizzle

                         Flatten

                         Flee

                         Flight

                         Fly

                         Fold

                         Fray

PART 4

Fates at Work

Gift from my dead siblings is familiarity with rituals:
slice, poison, radiate. Each with its own rhythm
spun through the MRI, tumours measured,
snip, snip of a bilateral mastectomy — the fates at work.

All painless, but for the removal of the drainage tubes
dangling like Xmas ornaments from my chest. Kind surgeon
used dissolving stitches, then packed the incision

with freezing for three days. Percocet sufficient
to end things three times over. I shut the door.

marked by a strip of horizontal tape where
breasts once hung, and pokey ribs now lift
toward sun. Shade is a reflexive bent

of shoulder inward and with small collapse of chest
I spiral round like a dog warming itself against
an unfamiliar cold. Yet labs run and roll, husky's

dive below the belly, while standard poodles leap,
bumping chests like soccer players or big horned sheep.

Now when hugging girlfriends, warmth
of mammalian flesh against bone
resolves my wonder that men hold tight.

Collapse

Crush

Unravel

not another camel in sight, your nostrils twitch
in the slackened air as you step offstage and carry
me out of the Süreyya Opera House nestled between

your breasted humps. Your steady gait, the lurch
and grate of the leather saddle, your rank coat wafts
assurance as we set sail over the dunes. (Even

my horoscope urged me to camel-up before
embarking). And as we ride, the frozen archipelago
of flesh — not me, but all of me that is left, softens.

I thread the needle of my eye, weave
and scissor a tapestry into your bristled coat
a map we trace for water, for light; perhaps

a treasured carpet our offspring will fly
through desert nights.

Even in the institution of cancer, there is hierarchy: better stage IV Hodgkin's Lymphoma than Stage I Lung. Treatment for thyroid? Will barely test your mettle. Just surgery? You lucky bastard. Surgery and rads? Straightforward. Ugh.

All three weapons deployed? Now you've arrived at the heart of the medical labyrinth! Ugly thing it is, and dull. Hungry, you offer blood. It butts with its horns, agitates. The conveyer belt of body parts picks up speed. You turn inside machines that launch you to the stars without a parachute.

Fly

Launch

Remove

Cornstalks in the First Freeze

Home to a headache more intense than ice cream.
They've injected epirubicin too quickly. *Five more
rounds?* Thighbones ache as blood burbles in

a chemical bath of Nupigen — faint echoes
of your pain. Reminds me of your nurse
the day after you died. Returning your supply
of the drug, she steps from behind her station,

Do you need a hug? Uh, actually no, I am OK.
Long, awkward pause. *Do you need one?*
Yes, she yips, and buries me.

Hair hurts — cornstalks in the first freeze,
silk tassels scatter on my shoulders.
Husband pulls out his scissors. Snip.

Next week, the clippers. *Buzzinga*
a post-industrial stroke of the Fates.
Refuge is a Buddhist self, though steroids
make chipmunk pouches of cheeks.

This naked orb is cool, alien. Fingers take
its measure. Fold it into my arm, breathe.

Perched on a kitchen stool, sun splits
the back deck. An involuntary yip
escapes her throat as hair clippers lick

her temples. Hair that was hurting,
bedding for a nest. Too toxic for birds?
Her husband's hand unwavering, shadows rise.

Rodin's Thinker? *No. No time. Sisyphus rolls,*
clinics to lab, scans to waiting rooms. Nurses'
spider fingers probe for veins.

Faint

Scatter

Snip

Limp as a dead guinea pig, a wig nests
in a cardboard casket swaddled in folds

of tissue. Fine as fishnet stockings, a woven cap
scoops the globe of her head,
a plastic buoy of synthetic hair is anchored.

Why this ritual? Why the cover? Staring
in the mirror, hands cover breasts, bush —
she has neither, naked, every limb, crook

a drowning rat swept along the gutter
clutching at any branch or rock: Nature shakes

her loose until shame is a newborn calf
lost amongst the legs of her maternal clan.
Trunks swing, we listen with our feet for home.

Invisible

while in treatment — did you feel this?
You never mentioned it. Back seeing
the oncologist six weeks after chemo.
She's royalty on hospital row, *but,* duly warned,

a hard-ass. All she wants to know of me
is the pathology report. Emitting not a whiff
of emotion, draped in a blue gown, I pick off bits
of lint. Her nose buried in my file, *We are coming*

up a year, have you scheduled your mammogram?
Um, no, I look down at my freshly, flattened chest.
More lint. Annoyed, her pantyhose chuffles.
Has your surgeon not scheduled a follow-up mammogram?

Papers flip with increasing vigour. About to open
the front of my gown, I lean in. *And what is there to scan?*
She looks up, cheeks a bracing red. Wily fox she is, takes

my typed list of vitamins and with a flick of her pen,
dismisses me. *You've misspelled this one.* Snip.

Flatten

Snip

Swaddle

Star Wars

All underground, walls the width of ancient castles,
I am lying in the bowels of the Starship Enterprise.
Tell me what you understand about your cancer,
the radiologist asks. He listens!

Co-ordinates checked and rechecked, measures I memorize
while lying here — *what else is one to do?* Challenge:
can I place myself perfectly on the table, neat
as a pole vaulter? Will never make the Olympics!

Bright green lasers, Northern lights. Zip, zap, zip zap,
every day for a month. Energy spins, stifles cellular chaos,
then stifles you. Afternoon naps lengthen with the spring sun.

A baby boa constrictor rests on the roof beam
of the gondola station. May he not shift and tumble
on my head. Below, roots of trees slither

above ground feeding off dying leaves. Green
to yellow to brown to green — Nature's daisy chain
knits decay to renewal. Howler monkeys,

three-toed sloths, gather aloft in tiered canopies
of emerald, chartreuse, jade, and lime. Poisonous
strawberry frogs, small as your baby toe, yowl,

defending their turf. Wary, I search
for vipers, thin as blades of grass along
my path, in the branches above.

Up, down, all around, nature's anarchy
without aim, but life itself: roar, pool, erode.
The waterfall does what waterfalls do.

Decay

Stifle

Tumble

It's not someone who's seen the light
it's a cold and it's a broken hallelujah.
—Leonard Cohen

Random rock and weed overlaid with a grid of pegs and string,
a loom hangs woolen against the sky.

A mother braids her daughter's hair, we brush aside
layers, wonder with Darwin at the beauty of the earthworm:
turning, digesting, preserving our history beneath their detritus.

Who discovered they were a protein of choice for fish?
How human of us to hang those who see our future

on the end of metal hooks. Hardly the reward they deserve
for endless buoys of hope they enfold creating a runway
to our past.

The song is on repeat. A misstep on the minor fall, I cannot
rise to the major lift. The Juno crowd cheers KD on
as if it were a Stanley Cup final. Her bare feet, she sways,

her voice — a blade's edge piercing our bafflement.
They rise to catch her. Ha —

Ever doubted the ecology of the body as metaphor for our earth
ship? You wilt as the alimentary canal reels with the toxins you
ingest. Keep the river moving! Infusion after infusion, you swim
to neutralize the cellular chaos, lap after lap. Nap after nap.

The soup in your head serves up limp vegetables. Eight months
pass without reading. You try a *New Yorker* essay and an hour later,
exhausted, you cannot recall the opening paragraph.

Daybed in the den, my refuge, three walls of windows open the
night lens. Moonlight in the trees, I search for raccoons, any life,
a breeze? Hope?

Only once did I ask myself if I wanted to join my dead family.
Clear as the call of our resident cardinal, a resounding *No* echoed
back.

A heron, sphinx-like in the reeds,
                          I fly deep to bones,
                                    tears grow flesh,
                                          keep me warm.

*After all the early Sunday morning rides, before trails teem
with weekend crowds and sun too high. After all the meals
hosted in our kitchens and on backyard decks.*

*After headwinds and rain, the chill of soaked feet,
the dehydration of too much heat, the chemical magic
of fireworks over the Falls has me believing in Star Wars.*

*After all the celebratory drinks, the crash and thrum of water
lulls us to sleep. We ride on the next day, pass vineyards and farms
through scorching heat, rain, freshly sprouted hair droops.*

*And just when you think you'll feel strong and brave, you collapse
into the chasm of what you have endured. The ocean wash
of endorphins recedes. After all, even cancer advertising lies.*

Note to Antigone — #4

Dear Tig:

Got my exit papers from the County of Cancer!
Empress signed off on October 18th. Walked
five kilometres east in the autumn light
over the valley where my brother lies.
Metal crosses anchored to either side
of the bridge, arms outstretched, ready
to catch those with an impulse to leap.

Lost, barnacled, rélés crawls onto
Dover beach as relish — whispered
as a wave surged over the deck.

French essences and quintesses ridicule
the English for their tasteless dishes that
condiments and jellies smear with flavour.

Queen of Condiments, I advise the nutritionist:
fridge shelves an army of glucose, fructose, potassium
sorbate, calcium chloride, tartrazie.

What is the colour of relish and betrayal?
It is 1594, King Lear's Gloucester is reading
a letter from Edgar to Edmund — his sons

plotting to overthrow him so their fortune might be
relished before they too become old and foolish!
Ha! The family pot comes to a boil.

Titillations of fresh garlic, ginger, lime, coriander,
tomato, chilies waft, arise from deep India and
envelope our limbic brains. You savour, turn

it over and over, on into the next day.

Grind

Hide

Illusion

Invisible

Lapse

Leak

Lean

Leave

Lose

Melt

Migrate

Perish

Poison

PART 5

Something Has Bitten Deep

Something has bitten deep into our family.
You will shake your head. Heavy as un-milked
udders, the rampage continues: packing for
Oban to pay homage to our ancestors,

husband goes down: low back pain, fatigue,
intermittent fevers mistaken for a spring day's
heat. Just finished two hundred kilometre cancer ride
in celebration of my recovery — of course we're

tired and sore! Harnessing my fear of being laughed
out of the ER — ha! Ten minutes, he's in line for a
CT Scan — Stage IV Hodgkin's lymphoma. Oncologist
thinks we should get a refund on our fundraising.

My boss, silent as a pyramid burial chamber when
I delay my return. Palliative care buddy calls
the cancer psychiatrist. He steps around
the curtain of my husband's hospital bed:

webs of fear and disbelief mesh, rip. A flailing
dolphin caught in tuna nets. No one knows
what to say to us. We are their worst nightmare,
a reminder of how wrong things can go even

when you are not avoiding Fate! *Spin, measure, snip!*
Three more weeks and eighteen diagnostics later, chemo.
Five days in ICU, bleomycin pulmonary toxicity
first round — *never seen this*, they shake their heads.

We watch numbers rise and fall. What they measure
we do not know. A Bach cantata? Mountainside ski runs?
Doctors come and go. To intubate or not to intubate?
That is the question.

Perched on a kitchen stool, summer sun splits
again. Clippers in hand, her husband's head
bowed. Unwavering, burnished steel blades
cross his scalp. Poised as a Buddhist monk.

Enfold

Envelop

Rip

Sun cracks the joint of water and sky
as we drive up the river valley, and
down the other side. Four stoplights

to the city's fury, spring's raw canopy
a green sieve, igniting the valley floor.
Alarmed by the vortex of wind and slope,
trees lean. Roots, over-worked quads
ache as earth gives way, limbs fall into
the arms of those who know the small
stray animal of the heart that makes
a shelter a home.

Arboreal prayers rise in the small whorls
of smoke for moms who leaned too far
calling them in from play.

Fly

Lean

Stray

*Late one spring, my brother drowned in the folds
of an embolism that blossomed unexpectedly
as he stood by the river surveying the horizon.
The ferry was on time, though we thought it early.*

*Next summer, my baby sister gave up the ocean
she'd just crossed. And, a month later, swimming
quietly as a goldfish, his memory just as short,
my dad kissed me one last time. Then my dog.*

*Six weeks later, a small leak in my vessel —
the horizon closed in, collapsing a year later
as my husband was ferried to the ICU.*

Will It Ever Stop

Your dear partner, sick again.
Your daughters brave.
Second time, gone are the ribbons
and cheerleading. They huddle.

Hospital calls — CT scan earlier
that day showing a blood clot
on husband's lung. *Will it blossom?*

Note to Antigone — #5

Dear Tig:

The only record of the County of Cancer close to your era rests
with Atossa, wife of Darius I and mother of Xerxes I. Had her
physician Democedes of Croton cut off her left breast,
a crabshell lump having grown within.

Of course the translation of the Greek words for *lesions* and
lumps is hotly debated. Can't imagine without anaesthetic!
Regardless, her words echo for both of us, do they not?

> *Long have I held my peace, as one struck dumb*
> *With sorrow. When so vast a thing is come*
> *Upon us, who can tell it, or who dare*
> *To ask the story? ... Yet, since man must bear*
> *What the gods send, be still, thou, and unroll —*
> *Albeit thy tears yet run — thine evil scroll*
> *To the utter end. Say first, who is not slain*
> *Of sceptered kings, and who shall ne'er again*
> *Look on this land, but leave an empty throne?*

Rumi lost his entire family. Meeting with the dervish
Shams-e-Tabrizi on 15 November 1244 completely
changed his life. An accomplished teacher and jurist, an ascetic.
Hmm, 768 years later, my birthday, what am I becoming?

Cornflower. Sea. Bruise deepens as black stains
blue. Light emerges through her milky pores —
a canvas jets paint with ribbons of white.
Sun radiates pink, yellow, across the shifting
vision. Blue quaffs black. Birds take flight
and weather plays. Dented by storms
black embraces blue again and again. Light
pours like fresh milk, refracting my sight.

Collapse

Leak

Quaff

All turning like a kaleidoscope — such whimsy —
you wake one day to find you've lost your love
of lime popsicles or black licorice. You can have it

all, though its time of arrival is uncertain and the one
who gives it may be entirely unexpected: remember
Aunt Doris and that diamond ring you admired?

My friend Georgia said she wanted to die fucking and she did,
at forty-eight, though she'd ingested a pharmaceutical rainbow
to deepen her elation. All and all at once?

All at once and for all time? Even Princess Di and John Jr
discovered life is shaped by angles and colours unimagined.
So if your judgement leads you astray, lay down your arms

before the stain of the day's sunset. Survey your orchard
of family, friends and colleagues, spread a blanket
as night falls. Tall grass our bed, all.

for you amongst the endless loops of memory: film clips, books, music, conversations, smiles.

Love overcomes fear: Antigone sneaks outside the city gates to bury her brother, a lone figure bent in grief by the desert winds, the scorching heat...

Love overcomes failure? I let them all down. So little time for ... my lack of courage to talk of final stages, a last voyage. My beloved... waited so patiently for me to return from caring for others when she needed me... a mind too broken to acknowledge our profound connection.

Ten years on, I am a child reading under the covers with a flashlight, sorting as one might a photo album, searching for words to hold you close. Knuckles whiten round the pen, steering through the hurricane. Can't breathe. Want to rest.

Antigone rolls the stone to seal her fate.
Her last thoughts? Suffering? Sorrow? Love?
Did Ismene keep vigil by her sister's grave?

No ink left.
You are gone, but it's not over...

Quit

Radiate

Recede

Reincarnate

Relinquish

Remove

Rot

Scatter

Secede

Sink

Slip

Split

Subside

Vacate

Vamoose

Wane

Wilt

Withdraw

PART 6

Fate's Fate — A Response to Antigonick

That was supposed to be my job — yes, there, the guy
wandering through the set with a measuring tape —
a stand-in for the Fates. Purely ironic? Man silenced?

We, my sisters and I, are woven through every
Greek story, and yet invisible. Now this asshole
with a measuring tape. Where's Spindle? Scissors?

Two-thirds of the story is missing! Is Fate's fate
to wander through this world in silence, unrecognized
for who she is: *the way of all flesh*?

Even now, man on the street recognizes
the names Apollo, Zeus — strutting about town
prize Dobermans. Maybe even Mighty Aphrodite?

(thank you, Woody Allen), but the Moirai?
Couldn't you give us our rightful place?

Fates' Fate — Let Me Try Again

We, who are mightier than the boys who warred;
the gods who screwed who they pleased. No, they
couldn't fuck us — and we, daughters of the Night,
the delimiters no one wants to hear from, much

less recognize. My namesakes. Fate of fates,
someone is having a last laugh. Antigone had
the conviction of her religious beliefs

so buried her brother's bones — screw the rule
of law as declared by Creon. But it cost her.
It cost the whole damn family — her fiancé,

her mother-in-law, old Creon. They all went
down, dear daughter of Oedipus and Jocasta.
Whatever became of Ismene?

Fates' Fate – Third Time's a Charm?

There is no escaping the final chaos.
If it was war and pestilence, revenge
and incest, that drove the Greeks,

today it is cancer. The Empress of all Maladies
whose very name creates panic,
stops us in our tracks.

Fates' Fate — Does a Fourth Response Make It Whole?

We sit in the surging chaos contemplating how
this came to be our measure — how we are going
to respond? Is there a path forward? Like a crab

on the beach, she slips behind rocks, dips into
the sand, invisible until she all but kills you.
The gnawing fatigue. You blame:

job, kids, mortgage, taxes, in-laws. We tie
ourselves in a net of constraints.
She, an unwanted houseguest who ignores all cues,

refuses to leave, then leaves the bed unmade. We
give her her due: a breast, a prostate, a lobe of lung
or liver. Our children marked to keep on giving,

their genetic fate a new measure as algorithms calculate
probabilities. A string of numbers I don't understand,
except they pull you along, into more knots of uncertainty.

OK, ovaries too — is that enough to let me pass?
Ah, passing — yes, well you'd think people would wear
their scars proudly, a badge of honour for having encountered

the Empress and survived. But no, made invisible again —
even when we give someone an extra measure — a second
chance, they hide — wigs, fake breasts, draping of all manner

disguising our deepest desire: to be known for who we are.
Here I am.

Notes

Pg. 26 — *My Brother's Bedside* — "Trostet, trostet meine Lieben" — trans., *Comfort me, comfort me my people.* Handel's Messiah (1741).

Pg. 28 — *See How Swiftly* — mindful of Don Cole's collection, *How We All Swiftly* (2005).

Pg. 42 — *I Wish That Hills and Mountains Were Behind Me?* St. John's Passion, Bach (1724).

Pg. 59 — *Paidos—Paraleipsis* — there is no noun for parents who have lost a child. Paidos in Greek — child's feet; paraleipsis — to be abandoned on this side.

Pg. 71 — *All the Tender Things* — January 29th, 2013 — John Hopkins Hospital (Baltimore, MD) conducted its first successful arm transplant on Brendan Morrocco, Iran war veteran.

Pg. 75 — *Diagnosis: Thanatosis* — "thanatosis" is a defence mechanism deployed by many a creature enabling them to fake their own death so to be left unharmed by predators. Challenge is, 20% die from doing this — they fake their death so well!

Pg. 79 — *Note to Antigone* — *#3* — Thank you to Dr. Siddhartha Mukherjee for his groundbreaking work, *The Emperor of All Maladies: A Biography of Cancer (2010).* Given the chaos and tangled-genetic-fated-ness of some cancers, the tangle of DNA, the overseer of this suffering felt more like an *empress* than the male counterpart.

Pg. 79 — *Land of Malady* and *County of Cancer* — phrases from Christopher Hitchens' *Mortality* (2012) — nouns and metaphors that let me laugh.

Pg. 85 — *On the Road to Damascus*: inspired by the sighting of a camel in a barnyard just outside Damascus, Ontario.

Pg. 101 — *Relish* — After visiting my nutritionist and taking stock of the refrigerator; then inspired by the French root of the English word 'relish' and *On Food and Cooking: The Science and Lore of the Kitchen* by Harold McGee (2004); King Lear, Act 1 Sc. ii Ll. 44–55, Shakespeare.

Pg. 104 — *Something Has Bitten Deep* — phrase from *Antigonick*, Anne Carson (2012).

Pg. 107 — *Rosedale Valley Commute* — Torontonians know this road well with seasonal inhabitants who claim this space for home.

Pg. 19, 57, 79, 100, 111 — *Notes To Antigone* — A.T. Sandison, *The First Recorded Case of Inflammatory Mastisis*. Queen Atossa, according to an anecdote of Herodotus (3.134.1–6), induced Darius to make war on the Greeks, because she wanted to have Attic, Argive, and Corinthian maidservants (see also Aelian, *Natura Animalium* 11.27). At her instigation a Persian expedition reconnoitered the Greek coasts and surveyed Greek naval power. It was guided by Democedes of Croton, her own and Darius' private physician.

Pg. 113 — Become the Sky — *Rumi* meets Shams-e-Tabrizi — from *Soul Fury: Rumi and Shams Tabriz on Friendship*, by Coleman Barks (2014).

Pg. 115 — *You Can Have It All* — a response to poem, *You Can't Have It All* by Barbara Ras in *Bite Every Sorrow (1998)*.

Pg. 121 — *Fate's Fate* — inspired by Anne Carson's *Antigonick* (2013) — enjoy the reading on YouTube.

Acknowledgements

It takes a village to see a writer through to the publication of a book.

Written in honour of my family members who faced the last leg of this life's journey with courage and love: Dad, Bruce, Nan & Sienna. For family that has endured.

Deepest love for Russell and Danna Symington-Ephland.

Heartfelt thanks to my editor, John Glenday, to Don Coles and Molly Peacock. For Monica Kidd, who brought her skilled poetic and medical vision to this story, working alongside as we edited and polished. A true friend to an emerging poet.

My healthcare team: Dr. Shelley Mclean, Dr. Wey-Liang Leong, Dr. Pamela Goodwin, Dr. Wilfred Levin, Dr. Jonathon Hunter, Dr. Michele Chaban, Velita Contiga RN, Anna Gormley RMT, Phil Rowe, trainer; and the YMCA of Greater Toronto;

Dear friends and colleagues for encouragement and support these past years, my gratitude. Too many to name, too frightened of inadvertently missing someone.

Poems, or versions of them, originally published in the following literary journals: *Under the Milkweed*, The New Quarterly, *Spring 2019; On the road to Damascus* and *Yoga Hangover,* Mojave River Review *(Fall/Winter Issue, 2018–19)*; *Cluster Fuck* and *Rituals of Hair*, Another Dysfunctional Cancer Poem Anthology, Mansfield Press, 2018; *Vanishing Acts: Descent*, Naugatauk River Review, Winter/Spring 2018; *Boreal Lungs*, Freefall Magazine, Fall 2016.

Bibliography

Carson, Anne. (2012). *Antigone*. New York, NY: New
    Directions Publishing.
University of Michigan, Ann Arbor performance with
    Juliette Binoche (2014).
Carson, Anne. (2010). *Antigonick*. New York, NY: New
    Directions Publishing.
Carson, Anne. *Nox* (2009). New York, NY: New Directions.
Curtis, Adam. (1998) *The Way of All Flesh* — On the
    Immortal Life of Henrietta Lacks (BBC documentary).
Deshazer, Mary K. (2005). *Fractured Borders, Reading Women's
    Cancer Literature*. Ann Arbor, MI: University of
    Michigan Press.
Gawande, Atule. (2014). *Being Mortal: Medicine and What
    Matters in the End*. London, UK: Picador Books.
Hitchens, Christopher. (2012). *Mortality*. New York, NY:
    Twelve Books Publishing.
Kalanithi, Paul. (2016) *When Breath Becomes Air*. New York,
    NY: Random House.
Maunder, Robert and Hunter, Jonathan. (2015). *Love, Fear
    and Health*. Toronto, ON: University of Toronto Press.
Moulds, Julia. (1998). *Woman With A Cubed Head*. Kalamazoo,
    MI: Western Michigan University Press.
Murkhajee, Siddartha. (2010). *The Emperor of All Maladies*.
    New York, NY: Simon & Shuster Inc.
Phillips, Adam. (2012). *Missing Out: In Praise of the Unlived Life*.
    New York, NY: New Directions Publishing.
Phillips, Adam. (1999). *Darwin's Worms*. London, UK: Faber and Faber
Ras, Barbara. (1998). *You Can Have It All* in Bite Every Sorrow.
    Baton Rouge, LA: Louisiana State University.
Skloot, Rebecca. (2010) *The Immortal Life of Henrietta Lacks*.
    New York, NY: Random House.
Wolfe, Virginia. (1930). *On Being Ill*. London, UK: Hogarth Press.
Yalom, Irvin R. (2008). *Staring at the Sun: Overcoming the Terror
    of Death*. San Francisco, CA: Jossey-Bass Publishers.

With deep artistic roots in dance, it is poetry that has wed Moira MacDougall's love of movement and rhythm with voice and linguistic performance. *Bone Dream* (Tightrope Books, 2009) was her first collection of poems. She is published in Canadian and US literary journals. Currently the Poetry Editor at the *Literary Review of Canada,* she resides in Toronto by the great lake.

MICHAEL RAFELSON